Louise Imogen Guiney

A roadside harp a book of verses

Louise Imogen Guiney

A roadside harp a book of verses

ISBN/EAN: 9783743328549

Manufactured in Europe, USA, Canada, Australia, Japa

Cover: Foto ©ninafisch / pixelio.de

Manufactured and distributed by brebook publishing software
(www.brebook.com)

Louise Imogen Guiney

A roadside harp a book of verses

A ROADSIDE HARP
A BOOK OF VERSES BY
LOUISE IMOGEN GUINEY

"Highway, since you my chief Parnassus be,
And that my Muse, to some ears not unsweet,
Tempers her words to trampling horses' feet,
More oft than to a chamber melody!"

BOSTON AND NEW YORK
HOUGHTON MIFFLIN AND
COMPANY   M DCCC XCIII

The Riverside Press, Cambridge, Mass., U. S. A.
Electrotyped and Printed by H. O. Houghton & Co.

TO DORA AND HESTER SIGERSON

There in the Druid brake
If the cuckoo be awake
Again, O take my rhyme!
And keep it long for the sake
Of a bygone primrose-time;
You of the star-bright head
That twilight thoughts sequester,
You to your native fountains led
Like to a young Muse garlanded:
Dora, and Hester.

March, 1893.

TABLE OF CONTENTS

A ROADSIDE HARP. POEMS
BY LOUISE IMOGEN GUINEY

I

THE mare is pawing by the oak,
  The chaise is cool and wide
For Peter Rugg the Bostonian
With his little son beside;
The women loiter at the wheels
In the pleasant summer-tide.

"And when wilt thou be home, Father?"
"And when, good husband, say:
The cloud hangs heavy on the house
What time thou art away."
He answers straight, he answers short,
"At noon of the seventh day."

"Fail not to come, if God so will,
And the weather be kind and clear."
"Farewell, farewell! But who am I
A blockhead rain to fear?
God willing or God unwilling,
I have said it, I will be here."

He gathers up the sunburnt boy
And from the gate is sped;
He shakes the spark from the stones below,

I

The bloom from overhead,
Till the last roofs of his own town
Pass in the morning-red.

Upon a homely mission
North unto York he goes,
Through the long highway broidered thick
With elder-blow and rose;
And sleeps in sound of breakers
At every twilight's close.

Intense upon his heedless head
Frowns Agamenticus,
Knowing of Heaven's challenger
The answer: even thus
The Patience that is hid on high
Doth stoop to master us.

II

Full light are all his parting dreams;
Desire is in his brain;
He tightens at the tavern-post
The fiery creature's rein:
"Now eat thine apple, six years' child!
We face for home again."

They had not gone a many mile
With nimble heart and tongue,
When the lone thrush grew silent
The walnut woods among;
And on the lulled horizon
A premonition hung.

2

The babes at Hampton schoolhouse,
The wife with lads at sea,
Search with a level-lifted hand
The distance bodingly;
And farmer folk bid pilgrims in
Under a safe roof-tree.

The mowers mark by Newbury
How low the swallows fly,
They glance across the southern roads
All white and fever-dry,
And the river, anxious at the bend,
Beneath a thinking sky.

But there is one abroad was born
To disbelieve and dare:
Along the highway furiously
He cuts the purple air.
The wind leaps on the startled world
As hounds upon a hare;

With brawl and glare and shudder ope
The sluices of the storm;
The woods break down, the sand upblows
In blinding volleys warm;
The yellow floods in frantic surge
Familiar fields deform.

From evening until morning
His skill will not avail,
And as he cheers his youngest born,
His cheek is spectre-pale;
For the bonnie mare from courses known
Has drifted like a sail!

3

On some wild crag he sees the dawn
Unsheathe her scimitar.
" Oh, if it be my mother-earth,
And not a foreign star,
Tell me the way to Boston,
And is it near or far? "

One watchman lifts his lamp and laughs :
" Ye 've many a league to wend."
The next doth bless the sleeping boy
From his mad father's end ;
A third upon a drawbridge growls :
" Bear ye to larboard, friend."

Forward and backward, like a stone
The tides have in their hold,
He dashes east, and then distraught
Darts west as he is told,
(Peter Rugg the Bostonian,
That knew the land of old !)

And journeying, and resting scarce
A melancholy space,
Turns to and fro, and round and round,
The frenzy in his face,
And ends alway in angrier mood,
And in a stranger place,

Lost ! lost in bayberry thickets
Where Plymouth plovers run,
And where the masts of Salem
Look lordly in the sun ;

Lost in the Concord vale, and lost
By rocky Wollaston!

Small thanks have they that guide him,
Awed and aware of blight;
To hear him shriek denial
It sickens them with fright:
" They lied to me a month ago
With thy same lie to-night! "

To-night, to-night, as nights succeed,
He swears at home to bide,
Until, pursued with laughter
Or fled as soon as spied,
The weather-drenchèd man is known
Over the country side!

IV

The seventh noon 's a memory,
And autumn 's closing in;
The quince is fragrant on the bough,
And barley chokes the bin.
" O Boston, Boston, Boston!
And O my kith and kin! "

The snow climbs o'er the pasture wall,
It crackles 'neath the moon;
And now the rustic sows the seed,
Damp in his heavy shoon;
And now the building jays are loud
In canopies of June.

For season after season
The three are whirled along,

5

Misled by every instinct
Of light, or scent, or song;
Yea, put them on the surest trail,
The trail is in the wrong.

Upon those wheels in any path
The rain will follow loud,
And he who meets that ghostly man
Will meet a thunder-cloud,
And whosoever speaks with him
May next bespeak his shroud.

Tho' nigh two hundred years have gone,
Doth Peter Rugg the more
A gentle answer and a true
Of living lips implore:
" Oh, show me to my own town,
And to my open door!"

V

Where shall he see his own town
Once dear unto his feet?
The psalms, the tankard to the King,
The beacon's cliffy seat,
The gabled neighborhood, the stocks
Set in the middle street?

How shall he know his own town
If now he clatters thro'?
Much men and cities change that have
Another love to woo;
And things occult, incredible,
They find to think and do.

6

With such new wonders since he went
A broader gossip copes,
Across the crowded triple hills,
And up the harbor slopes,
Tradition's self for him no more
Remembers, watches, hopes.

But ye, O unborn children!
(For many a race must thrive
And drip away like icicles
Ere Peter Rugg arrive,)
If of a sudden to your ears
His plaint is blown alive;

If nigh the city, folding in
A little lad that cries,
A wet and weary traveller
Shall fix you with his eyes,
And from the crazy carriage lean
To spend his heart in sighs:—

" That I may enter Boston,
Oh, help it to befall!
There would no fear encompass me,
No evil craft appall;
Ah, but to be in Boston,
GOD WILLING, after all!"—

Ye children, tremble not, but go
And lift his bridle brave
In the one Name, the dread Name,
That doth forgive and save,
And lead him home to Copp's Hill ground,
And to his fathers' grave.

"In Clent cow-batch, Kenelm King born
Lieth under a thorn."

I T was a goodly child,
Sweet as the gusty May;
It was a knight that broke
On his play,
A fair and coaxing knight:
"O little liege!" said he,
"Thy sister bids thee come
After me.

"A pasture rolling west
Lies open to the sun,
Bright-shod with primroses
Doth it run;
And forty oaks be nigh,
Apart, and face to face,
And cow-bells all the morn
In the space.

"And there the sloethorn bush
Beside the water grows,
And hides her mocking head
Under snows;
Black stalks afoam with bloom,
And never a leaf hath she:
Thou crystal of the realm,
Follow me!"

Uplooked the undefiled:
"All things, ere I was born
My sister found; now find
Me the thorn."

They travelled down the lane,
An hour's dust they made:
The belted breast of one
Bore a blade.

The primroses were out,
The aislèd oaks were green,
The cow-bells pleasantly
Tinked between;
The brook was beaded gold,
The thorn was burgeoning,
Where evil Ascobert
Slew the King.

He hid him in the ground,
Nor washed away the dyes,
Nor smoothed the fallen curls
From his eyes.
No father had the babe
To bless his bed forlorn;
No mother now to weep
By the thorn.

There fell upon that place
A shaft of heavenly light;
The thorn in Mercia spake
Ere the night:
" Beyond, a sister sees
Her crownèd period,
But at my root a lamb
Seeth God."

Unto each, even so.
As dew before the cloud,

9

The guilty glory passed
Of the proud.
Boy Kenelm has the song,
Saint Kenelm has the bower;
His thorn a thousand years
Is in flower!

❧

I

THE wheels are silent, the cords are slack,
The terrible faces are surging back.
France, they too love thee! bid that keep plain;

The wrath and carnage I stayed afar
Colleagues of my white conscience are :
Accept my slayers, accept me slain !

Shed for days, in its olden guise
The quiet delicate snake-skin lies
To cheat a boy on his woodland stroll :

What if he crush it?   Others see
Beauty's miracle under a tree
Supple in mail, and adroit, and whole;

The shaper rid of a shape, and thence
(Growth of an outgrown excellence),
Mounted with infinite might and speed,

Freed like a soul to the heaven it dreamed;
Over life that was, and death that seemed
A victory and a revenge indeed !

As the serpent moves to the open spring,
The while a mock, a delusive thing
Sole in sight of the crowd may be,

So ye, my martyrs, arise, advance!
For what is left at the feet of France
It is our failure, it is not we.

II

Not to ourselves our strength we brought:
Inexpiable the Hand that wrought
In us the ruin of no redress,

The storm, the effort, the pang, the fire,
The premonition, the vast desire,
The primal passion of righteousness!

Scarce by the pitiful thwarted plan,
The haste, or the studious fears of man
Drawing a discord from best delight,

The measure is meted of God most wise;
Nor the future, with her adjusted eyes,
Shall speak us false in our dying fight.

But e'en to me now some use is clear
In the builded truth down-beaten here
For any along the way to spurn,

Since ever our broken task may stand
Disaster's college in one saved land,
Whence many a stripling state shall learn.

Vergniaud in the Tumbril Out of the human shoots the divine :
Be the Republic our only sign,
For whose life's glory our lives have been

Ambassadors on a noble way
Tempest-driven, and sent astray
The first and the final good between.

Close to the vision undestroyed,
The hope not compassed and yet not void,
We perish so ; but the world shall mark

On the hilltop of our work we died,
With joy of the groom before the bride,
With a dawn-cry thro' the battle's dark.

III

O last save me on the scaffold's round !
Take heart, that after a thirst profound
The cup of delicious death is near,

And whoso hold it, or whence it flow,
O drink it to France, to France ! and know
For the gift thou givest, thou hast her tear.

True seed thou wert of the sunnier hour,
Honorable, and burst to flower
Late in a hell-pit poison-walled :

Farewell, mortality lopped and pale,
Thou body that wast my friend ! and Hail,
Dear spirit already ! . . . My name is called.

12

HOW tender and how slow, in sunset's
  cheer,
Far on the hill, our quiet treetops fade!
A broidery of northern seaweed, laid
Long in a book, were scarce more fine and
  clear.
Frost, and sad light, and windless atmosphere
Have breathed on them, and of their frailties
  made
Beauty more sweet than summer's builded
  shade,
Whose green domes fall, to bring this wonder
  here.
O ye forgetting and outliving boughs,
With not a plume, gay in the jousts before,
Left for the Archer! so, in evening's eye,
So stilled, so lifted, let your lover die,
Set in the upper calm no voices rouse,
Stript, meek, withdrawn, against the heavenly
  door.

GOOD oars, for Arnold's sake
  By Laleham lightly bound,
And near the bank, O soft,
Darling swan!
Let not the o'erweary wake
From this his natal ground,
But where he slumbered oft,
Slumber on.

W. H.
1778-1830

BETWEEN the wet trees and the sorry
        steeple,
Keep, Time, in dark Soho, what once was
        Hazlitt,
Seeker of Truth, and finder oft of Beauty;

Beauty's a sinking light, ah, none too faithful;
But Truth, who leaves so here her spent pursuer,
Forgets not her great pawn: herself shall claim
        it.

Therefore sleep safe, thou dear and battling
        spirit,
Safe also on our earth, begetting ever
Some one love worth the ages and the nations!

Nothing falls under to thine eyes eternal.
Sleep safe in dark Soho: the stars are shining,
Titian and Wordsworth live; the People
        marches.

&

The Vigil-
at-Arms

KEEP holy watch with silence, prayer, and
        fasting
Till morning break, and all the bugles play;
Unto the One aware from everlasting
Dear are the winners: thou art more than
        they.

Forth from this peace on manhood's way thou
        goest,
Flushed with resolve, and radiant in mail;
Blessing supreme for men unborn thou sowest,
O knight elect! O soul ordained to fail!

L ET thoughts go hence as from a mountain
    spring,   *A Madon-*
                          na of Do-
Of the great dust of battle clean and whole, *menico*
And the wild birds that have no nest nor goal *Ghirlan-*
Fold in a young man's breast their trancèd *dajo*
    wing ;
For thou art made of purest Light, a thing
Art gave, beyond her own devout control ;
And Light upon thy seeing, suffering soul
Hath wrought a sign for many journeying;
Our sign. As up a wayside, after rain,
When the blown beeches purple all the height
And clouds sink to the sea-marge, suddenly
The autumn sun (how soft, how solemn-bright !)
Moves to the vacant dial, so is lain
God's meaning Hand, thou chosen, upon thee.

A PRIL is sad, as if the end she knew.   *Spring*
  The maple's misty red, the willow's gold *Nightfall*
Face-deep in nimble water, seem to hold
In hope's own weather their autumnal hue.
There is no wind, no star, no sense of dew,
But the thin vapors gird the mountain old,
And the moon, risen before the west is cold,
Pale with compassion slopes into the blue.
Under the shining dark the day hath passed
Shining ; so even of thee was home bereaved,
Thou dear and pensive spirit ! overcast
Hardly at all, but drawn from light to light,
Who in the doubtful hour, and unperceived,
Rebuked adoring hearts with change and
    flight.

THE breath of dew, and twilight's grace,
Be on the lonely battle-place;
And to so young, so kind a face,
The long, protecting grasses cling!
(Alas, alas,
The one inexorable thing!)

In rocky hollows cool and deep,
The bees our boyhood hunted sleep;
The early moon from Ida's steep
Comes to the empty wrestling-ring.
(Alas, alas,
The one inexorable thing!)

Upon the widowed wind recede
No echoes of the shepherd's reed,
And children without laughter lead
The war-horse to the watering.
(Alas, alas,
The one inexorable thing!)

Thou stranger Ajax Telamon!
What to the loveliest hast thou done,
That ne'er with him a maid may run
Across the marigolds in spring?
(Alas, alas,
The one inexorable thing!)

With footstep separate and slow
The father and the mother go,
Not now upon an urn they know
To mingle tears for comforting.
(Alas, alas,
The one inexorable thing!)

The world to me has nothing dear
Beyond the namesake river here:
O Simois is wild and clear!
And to his brink my heart I bring;
(Alas, alas,
The one inexorable thing!)

My heart no more, if that might be,
Would stay his waters from the sea,
To cover Troy, to cover me,
To save us from the perishing.
(Alas, alas,
The one inexorable thing!)

❧

FOLLY and Time have fashioned
   Of thee a songless reed;
O not-of-earth-impassioned!
   Thy music's mute indeed.

Red from the chantry crannies
   The orchids burn and swing,
And where the arch began is
   Rest for a raven's wing;

And up the bossy column
   Quick tails of squirrels wave,
And black, prodigious, solemn,
   A forest fills the nave.

Still faithfuller, still faster,
   To ruin give thy heart:

Perfect before the Master
Aye as thou wert, thou art.

But I am wind that passes
In ignorant wild tears,
Uplifted from the grasses,
Blown to the void of years,

Blown to the void, yet sighing
In thee to merge and cease,
Last breath of beauty's dying,
Of sanctity, of peace!

Tho' use nor place forever
Unto my soul befall,
By no belovèd river
Set in a saintly wall,

Do thou by builders given
Speech of the dumb to be,
Beneath thine open heaven,
Athassel! pray for me.

❧

Florentin

H EART all full of heavenly haste, too like
the bubble bright
On loud little water floating half of an April
night,
Fled from the ear in music, fled from the eye
in light,

Dear and stainless heart of a boy! No Florentin
     sweeter thing can be
Drawn to the quiet centre of God who is our sea;
Whither, thro' troubled valleys, we also follow
     thee.

❧

I

WE chose the faint chill morning, friend *Friendship*
    and friend,   *Broken*
Pacing the twilight out beneath an oak,
Soul calling soul to judgment; and we spoke
Strange things and deep as any poet penned,
Such truth as never truth again can mend,
Whatever arts we win, what gods invoke;
It was not wrath, it made nor strife nor
     smoke:
Be what it may, it had a solemn end.
Farewell, in peace. We of the selfsame
     throne
Are foeman vassals; pale astrologers,
Each a wise sceptic of the other's star.
Silently, as we went our ways alone,
The steadfast sun, whom no poor prayer de-
     ters,
Drew high between us his majestic bar.

II

Mine was the mood that shows the dearest
     face
Thro' a long avenue, and voices kind
Idle, and indeterminate, and blind

19

Friendship Broken As rumors from a very distant place;
Yet, even so, it gathered the first chase
Of the first swallows where the lane's in-
        clined,
An ebb of wavy wings to serve my mind
For round Spring's vision. Ah, some equal
        grace
(The calm sense of seen beauty without sight)
Befell thee, honorable heart! no less
In patient stupor walking from the dawn;
Albeit thou too wert loser of life's light,
Like fallen Adam in the wilderness,
Aware of naught but of the thing withdrawn.

❦

A Song of the Lilac ABOVE the wall that's broken,
And from the coppice thinned,
So sacred and so sweet
The lilac in the wind!
And when by night the May wind blows
The lilac-blooms apart,
The memory of his first love
Is shaken on his heart.

In tears it long was buried,
And trances wrapt it round;
O how they wake it now,
The fragrance and the sound!
For when by night the May wind blows
The lilac-blooms apart,
The memory of his first love
Is shaken on his heart.

KEEP of the Norman, old to flood and cloud!
Thou dost reproach me with thy sunset look,
That in our common menace, I forsook
Hope, the last fear, and stood impartial proud:
Almost, almost, while ether spake aloud,
Death from the smoking stones my spirit
      shook
Into thy hollow as leaves into a brook,
No more than they by heaven's assassins cowed.

But now thy thousand-scarrèd steep is flecked
With the calm kisses of the light delayed,
Breathe on me better valor: to subject
My soul to greed of life, and grow afraid
Lest, ere her fight's full term, the Architect
See downfall of the stronghold that He made.

❧

IN a new poet's and a new friend's honor,
  Forth from the scornèd town and her gold-
      getting,
Come men with lutes and bowls, and find a
      welcome
Here in my garden,

Find bowers and deep shade and windy
      grasses,
And by the south wall, wet and forward-jut-
      ting,
One early branch fire-tipped with Roman
      cherries.
O naught is absent,

21

O naught but you, kind head that far in prison
Sunk on a weary arm, feels no god's pity
Stroking and sighing where the kingly laurels
Were once so plenty,

Nor dreams, from revels and strange faces
        turning,
How on the strength of my fair tree that knew
        you,
I lean to-day, when most my heart is laden
With your rich verses!

Since, long ago, in other gentler weather
Ere wrath and exile were, you lay beneath it,
(Your symbol then, your innocent wild brother,
Glad with your gladness,)

What has befallen in the world of wonder,
That still it puts forth bubbles of sweet color,
And you, and you that burst our eyes with
        beauty,
Are sapped and rotten?

Alas! When my young guests have done with
        singing,
I break it, leaf and fruit, my garden's glory,
And hold it high among them, and say after:
" O my poor Ovid,

" Years pass, and loves pass too; and yet re-
        member
For the clear time when we were boys together,
These tears at home are shed; and with you also
Your bough is dying."

I

I KNEAD and I spin, but my life is low the
while,
Oh, I long to be alone, and walk abroad a mile,
Yet if I walk alone, and think of naught at
all,
Why from me that's young should the wild
tears fall?

The shower-stricken earth, the earth-colored
streams,
They breathe on me awake, and moan to me
in dreams,
And yonder ivy fondling the broke castle-wall,
It pulls upon my heart till the wild tears fall.

The cabin-door looks down a furze-lighted hill,
And far as Leighlin Cross the fields are green
and still;
But once I hear the blackbird in Leighlin
hedges call,
The foolishness is on me, and the wild tears
fall!

II

'T is the time o' the year, if the quicken-bough
be staunch,
The green, like a breaker, rolls steady up the
branch,
And surges in the spaces, and floods the trunk,
and heaves
In little angry spray that is the under-white of
leaves;

23

And from the thorn in companies the foamy
    petals fall,
And waves of jolly ivy wink along a windy
    wall.

'T is the time o' the year the marsh is full of
    sound,
And good and glorious it is to smell the living
    ground.
The crimson-headed catkin shakes above the
    pasture-bars,
The daisy takes the middle field and spangles
    it with stars,
And down the bank into the lane the prim-
    roses do crowd,
All colored like the twilight moon, and spread-
    ing like a cloud!

'T is the time o' the year, in early light and
    glad,
The lark has a music to drive a lover mad;
The downs are dripping nightly, the breathèd
    damps arise,
Deliciously the freshets cool the grayling's
    golden eyes,
And lying in a row against the chilly north,
    the sheep
Inclose a place without a wind for tender
    lambs to sleep.

'T is the time o' the year I turn upon the
    height
To watch from my harrow the dance of going
    light;

And if before the sun be hid, come slowly up
    the vale
Honora with her dimpled throat, Honora with
    her pail,
Hey, but there's many a March for me, and
    many and many a lass!
I fall to work and song again, and let Honora
    pass.

ALL summer the breath of the roses around *The Japa-*
  Exhales with a delicate, passionate sound; *nese Anem-*
one
And when from a trellis, in holiday places,
They croon and cajole, with their slumberous
    faces,
A lad in the lane must slacken his paces.

Fragrance of these is a voice in a bower:
But low by the wall is my odorless flower,
So pure, so controlled, not a fume is above her,
That poet or bee should delay there and hover;
For she is a silence, and therefore I love her.

And never a mortal by morn or midnight
Is called to her hid little house of delight;
And she keeps from the wind, on his pillages
    olden,
Upon a true stalk in rough weather upholden,
Her winter-white gourd with the hollow moon-
    golden.

While ardors of roses contend and increase,
Methinks she has found how noble is peace,

Like a spirit besought from the world to dis-
        sever,
Not absent to men, tho' resumed by the Giver,
And dead long ago, being lovely for ever.

❧

THE Ox he openeth wide the Doore
    And from the Snowe he calls her inne,
And he hath seen her Smile therefore,
Our Ladye without Sinne.
Now soone from Sleepe
A Starre shall leap,
And soone arrive both King and Hinde;
Amen, Amen:
But O, the place co'd I but finde!

The Ox hath husht his voyce and bent
Trewe eyes of Pitty ore the Mow,
And on his lovelie Neck, forspent,
The Blessed lays her Browe.
Around her feet
Full Warme and Sweete
His bowerie Breath doth meeklie dwell;
Amen, Amen:
But sore am I with Vaine Travèl!

The Ox is host in Juda's stall,
And Host of more than onelie one,
For close she gathereth withal
Our Lorde her littel Sonne.
Glad Hinde and King
Their Gyfte may bring

But wo'd to-night my Teares were there, *Tryste*
Amen, Amen: *Noel*
Between her Bosom and His hayre!

❧

TAKE Temperance to thy breast, *A Talis-*
  While yet is the hour of choosing, *man*
As arbitress exquisite
Of all that shall thee betide ;
For better than fortune's best
Is mastery in the using,
And sweeter than anything sweet
The art to lay it aside !

❧

NO round boy-satyr, racing from the mere, *Heathen-*
  Shakes on the mountain-lawn his drip- *esse*
      ping head
This many a May, your sister being dead,
Ye Christian folk ! your sister great and dear.
To breathe her name, to think how sad-sin-
      cere
Was all her searching, straying, dreaming,
      dread,
How of her natural night was Plato bred,
A star to keep the ways of honor clear,
Who will not sigh for her ? who can forget
Not only unto campèd Israel,
Nor martyr-maids that as a bridegroom met
The Roman lion's roar, salvation fell ?
To Him be most of praise that He is yet
Your God thro' gods not inaccessible.

27

WHAT trout shall coax the rod of yore
    In Itchen stream to dip?
What lover of her banks restore
    That sweet Socratic lip?
    Old fishing and wishing
    Are over many a year.
O hush thee, O hush thee! heart innocent and
      dear.

Again the foamy shallows fill,
    The quiet clouds amass,
And soft as bees by Catherine Hill
    At dawn the anglers pass,
    And follow the hollow,
    In boughs to disappear.
O hush thee, O hush thee! heart innocent and
      dear.

Nay, rise not now, nor with them take
    One silver-freckled fool!
Thy sons to-day bring each an ache
    For ancient arts to cool.
    But, father, lie rather
    Unhurt and idle near;
O hush thee, O hush thee! heart innocent and
      dear.

While thought of thee to men is yet
    A sylvan playfellow,
Ne'er by thy marble they forget
    In pious cheer to go.
    As air falls, the prayer falls
    O'er kingly Winchester:
O hush thee, O hush thee! heart innocent and
      dear.   28

THIS was the truest man of men,
   The early-armored citizen,
Who had, with most of sight,
Most passion for the right;

Who first forecasting treason's scope
Able to sap the Founders' hope,
First to the laic arm
Cried ultimate alarm;

Who bent upon his guns the while
A misconceived and aching smile,
And felt, thro' havoc's part,
A torment of the heart,

Sure, when he cut the moated South
From Shiloh to Savannah's mouth,
Braved grandly to the end,
To conquer like a friend;

In whom the Commonwealth withstood
Again the Carolinian blood,
The beautiful proud line
Beneath an evil sign,

And taught his foes and doubters still
How fatal is a good man's will,
That like a sun or sod
Thinks not itself, but God!

Many the captains of our wrath
Sought thus the pious civic path,
Knowing in what a land
Their destiny was planned,

29

And after, with a forward sense,
A simple Roman excellence,
Pledge in their spirit bore
That war should be no more.

Thrice Roman he, who saw the shock
(Calm as a weather-wrinkled rock,)
Roll in the Georgian fen ;
And steadfast aye as then

In plenitude of old control
That asked, secure of his own soul,
No pardon and no aid,
If clear his way were made,

Would have nor seat nor bays, nor bring
The Cæsar in him to be king,
But with abstracted ear
Rode pleased without a cheer.

Now he declines from peace and age,
And home, his triple heritage,
The last and dearest head
Of all our perfect dead,

O what if sorrow cannot reach
Far in the shallow fords of speech,
But leads us silent round
The sad Missouri ground,

Where on her hero Freedom lays
The scroll and blazon of her praise,
And bids to him belong
Arms trailing, and a song,

And broken flags with ruined dyes
(Bright once in young and dying eyes),
Against the morn to shake
For love's familiar sake?

The blessèd broken flags unfurled
Above a healed and happier world!
There let them droop, and be
His tent of victory;

There, in each year's auguster light,
Lean in, and loose their red and white,
Like apple-blossoms strewn
Upon his burial-stone.

For nothing more, the ages thro',
Can nature or the nation do
For him who helped retrieve
Our life, as we believe,

Save that we also, trooping by
In sound yet of his battle-cry,
Safeguard with general mind
Our pact as brothers kind,

And, ever nearer to our star,
Adore indeed not what we are,
But wise reprovings hold
Thankworthier than gold;

And bear in faith and rapture such
As can eternal issues touch,
Whole from the final field,
Our father Sherman's shield.

WHEN on the marge of evening the last
blue light is broken,
And winds of dreamy odor are loosened from
afar,
Or when my lattice opens, before the lark has
spoken,
On dim laburnum - blossoms, and morning's
dying star,

I think of thee, (O mine the more if other eyes
be sleeping !)
Whose great and noonday splendor the many
share and see,
While sacred and forever, some perfect law is
keeping
The late and early twilight alone and sweet for
me.

THRO' rosy cloud, and over thorny towers,
Their wings with all the autumn distance
filled,
From Isis' valley border hundred-hilled,
The rooks are crowding home as evening low-
ers :
Not for men only and their musing hours,
By battled walls did gracious Wykeham build
These dewy spaces early sown and stilled,
These dearest inland melancholy bowers.

Blest birds ! A book held open on the knee
Below, is all they know of Adam's blight :
With surer art the while, and simpler rite,

32

They follow Truth in some monastic tree, *Rooks in New College Gardens*
Where breathe against their innocent breasts
     by night
The scholar's star, the star of sanctity.

❦

O PEN, Time, and let him pass *Open, Time*
   Shortly where his feet would be!
Like a leaf at Michaelmas
Swooning from the tree,

Ere its hour the manly mind
Trembles in a sure decrease,
Nor the body now can find
Any hold on peace.

Take him, weak and overworn;
Fold about his dying dream
Boyhood, and the April morn,
And the rolling stream:

Weather on a sunny ridge,
Showery weather, far from here;
Under some deep-ivied bridge,
Water rushing clear:

Water quick to cross and part,
(Golden light on silver sound),
Weather that was next his heart
All the world around!

Soon upon his vision break
These, in their remembered blue;

33

Open, Time He shall toil no more, but wake
Young, in air he knew.

He has done with roofs and men.
Open, Time, and let him pass,
Vague and innocent again,
Into country grass.

❦

*The
Knight
Errant
(Dona-
tello's
Saint
George)*
SPIRITS of old that bore me,
And set me, meek of mind,
Between great dreams before me,
And deeds as great behind,
Knowing humanity my star
As first abroad I ride,
Shall help me wear, with every scar,
Honor at eventide.

Let claws of lightning clutch me
From summer's groaning cloud,
Or ever malice touch me,
And glory make me proud.
O give my youth, my faith, my sword,
Choice of the heart's desire:
A short life in the saddle, Lord!
Not long life by the fire.

Forethought and recollection
Rivet mine armor gay!
The passion for perfection
Redeem my failing way!

34

The arrows of the tragic time
From sudden ambush cast,
With calm angelic touches ope
My Paradise at last !

I fear no breathing bowman,
But only, east and west,
The awful other foeman
Impowered in my breast.
The outer fray in the sun shall be,
The inner beneath the moon ;
And may Our Lady'lend to me
Sight of the Dragon soon!

❦

THE gusty morns are here,
   When all the reeds ride low with level
      spear ;
And on such nights as lured us far of yore,
Down rocky alleys yet, and thro' the pine,
The Hound-star and the pagan Hunter shine:
But I and thou, ah, field-fellow of mine,
Together roam no more.

Soft showers go laden now
With odors of the sappy orchard-bough,
And brooks begin to brawl along the march ;
The late frost steams from hollow sedges high;
The finch is come, the flame-blue dragon-fly,
The cowslip's common gold that children spy,
The plume upon the larch.

There is a music fills
The oaks of Belmont and the Wayland hills
Southward to Dewing's little bubbly stream,
The heavenly weather's call! Oh, who alive
Hastes not to start, delays not to arrive,
Having free feet that never felt a gyve
Weigh, even in a dream?

But thou, instead, hast found
The sunless April uplands underground,
And still, wherever thou art, I must be.
My beautiful! arise in might and mirth,
For we were tameless travellers from our birth;
Arise against thy narrow door of earth,
And keep the watch for me.

❦

SHE alone of Shepherdesses
With her blue disdayning eyes,
Wo'd not hark a Kyng that dresses
All his lute in sighes:
Yet to winne
Katheryn,
I elect for mine Emprise.

None is like her, none above her,
Who so lifts my youth in me,
That a littel more to love her
Were to leave her free!
But to winne
Katheryn,
Is mine utmost love's degree.

36

Distaunce, cold, delay, and danger,
Build the four walles of her bower;
She's noe Sweete for any stranger,
She's noe valley flower:
And to winne
Katheryn,
To her height my heart can Tower!

Uppe to Beautie's promontory
I will climb, nor loudlie call
Perfect and escaping glory
Folly, if I fall:
Well to winne
Katheryn!
To be worth her is my all.

❦

I

IMPERIAL Iffley, Cumnor bowered in
    green,
And Templar Sandford in the boatman's
    call,
And sweet-belled Appleton, and Wytham
    wall
That doth upon adoring ivies lean;
Meek Binsey; Dorchester where streams con-
    vene
Bidding on graves her solemn shadow fall;
Clear Cassington that soars perpetual;
Holton and Hampton, and ye towers between:
If one of all in your sad courts that come,
Belovèd and disparted! be your own,
Kin to the souls ye had, while time endures,

*On the Pre-
Reforma-
tion
Churches
about Ox-
ford*

37

On the Pre-
Reforma-
tion
Churches
about Ox-
ford Known to each exiled, each estrangèd stone
Home in the quarries of old Christendom, —
Ah, mark him : he will lay his cheek to yours.

II

Is this the end? is this the pilgrim's day
For dread, for dereliction, and for tears?
Rather, from grass and air and many spheres
In prophecy his spirit sinks away ;
And under English eaves, more still than
      they,
Far-off, incoming, wonderful, he hears
The long-arrested and believing years
Carry the sea-wall!   Shall he, sighing, say,
" Farewell to Faith, for she is dead at best
Who had such beauty "? or with kisses lain
For witness on her darkened doors, go by
With a new psalm: "O banished light so
      nigh!
Of them was I who bore thee and who blest;
Even here remember me when thou shalt
      reign."

❦

The Still of
the Year U P from the willow-root
   Subduing agonies leap;
The squirrel and the purple moth
Turn over amid their sleep;
The icicled rocks aloft
Burn saffron and blue alway,
And trickling and tinkling
The snows of the drift decay.
O mine is the head must hang

38

And share the immortal pang !
Winter or spring is fair ;
Thaw 's hard to bear.
Heigho ! my heart 's sick.

Sweet is cherry-time, sweet
A shower, a bobolink,
And the little trillium-blossom
Tucked under her leaf to think;
But here in the vast unborn
Is the bitterest place to be,
Till striving and longing
Shall quicken the earth and me.
What change inscrutable
Is nigh us, we know not well ;
Gone is the strength to sigh
Either to live or die.
Heigho ! my heart 's sick.

❦

TRUE love's own talisman, which here
   Shakespeare and Sidney failed to teach,
A steel-and-velvet Cavalier
Gave to our Saxon speech :

Chief miracle of theme and touch
That upstart enviers adore :
*I could not love thee, dear, so much,
Loved I not Honour more.*

No critic born since Charles was king
But sighed in smiling, as he read :

39

" Here 's theft of the supremest thing
A poet might have said ! "

Young knight and wit and beau, who won
Mid war's adventure, ladies' praise,
Was 't well of you, ere you had done,
To blight our modern bays ?

O yet to you, whose random hand
Struck from the dark whole gems like these,
Archaic beauty, never planned
Nor reared by wan degrees,

Which leaves an artist poor, and art
An earldom richer all her years ;
To you, dead on your shield apart,
Be " Ave ! " passed in tears.

How shall this singing era spurn
Her master, and in lauds be loath ?
Your worth, your work, bid us discern
Light exquisite in both.

'T was virtue's breath inflamed your lyre,
Heroic from the heart it ran ;
Nor for the shedding of such fire
Lives since a manlier man.

And till your strophe sweet and bold
So lovely aye, so lonely long,
Love's self outdo, dear Lovelace ! hold
The pinnacles of song.

FRIEND who hast gone, and dost enrich *T. W. P.*
    to-day *1819-1892*
New England brightly building far away,
And crown her liberal walk
With company more choice, and sweeter talk,

Look not on Fame, but Peace; and in a bower
Receive at last her fulness and her power:
Nor wholly, pure of heart!
Forget thy few, who would be where thou art.

❦

WAITING on Him who knows us and our *Summum*
    need, *Bonum*
Most need have we to dare not, nor desire,
But as He giveth, softly to suspire
Against His gift, with no inglorious greed,
For this is joy, tho' still our joys recede;
And, as in octaves of a noble lyre,
To move our minds with His, and clearer,
    higher,
Sound forth our fate; for this is strength
    indeed.

Thanks to His love let earth and man dis-
    pense
In smoke of worship when the heart is stillest,
A praying more than prayer: "Great good
    have I,
Till it be greater good to lay it by;
Nor can I lose peace, power, permanence,
For these smile on me from the thing Thou
    willest!"

THE spacious open vale, the vale of doom,
Is full of autumn sunset; blue and strong
The semicirque of water sweeps among
Her lofty acres, each a martyr's tomb;
And slowly, slowly, melt into the gloom
Two little idling clouds, that look for long
Like roseleaf bodies of two babes in song
Correggio left to flush a convent room.

Dear hill deflowered in the frantic war!
In my day, rather, have I seen thee blest
With pastoral roofs to break the darker crest
Of apple-woods by many-islèd Loire,
And fires that still suffuse the lower west,
Blanching the beauty of thine evening star.

❧

JAR in arm, they bade him rove
Thro' the alder's long alcove,
Where the hid spring musically
Gushes to the ample valley.
(There's a bird on the under bough
Fluting evermore and now:
" Keep — young!" but who knows how?)

Down the woodland corridor,
Odors deepened more and more;
Blossomed dogwood, in the briers,
Struck her faint delicious fires;
Miles of April passed between
Crevices of closing green,
And the moth, the violet-lover,
By the wellside saw him hover.

42

Ah, the slippery sylvan dark!
Never after shall he mark
Noisy ploughmen drinking, drinking,
On his drownèd cheek down-sinking;
Quit of serving is that wild,
Absent, and bewitchèd child,
Unto action, age, and danger,
Thrice a thousand years a stranger.

Fathoms low, the naiads sing
In a birthday welcoming;
Water-white their breasts, and o'er him,
Water-gray, their eyes adore him.
(There's a bird on the under bough
Fluting evermore and now:
"Keep—young!" but who knows how?)

❦

THE sun that hurt his lovers from on high   *Nocturne*
Is fallen; she more merciful is nigh,
The blessèd one whose beauty's even glow
Gave never wound to any shepherd's eye.
Above our pausing boat in shallows drifted,
Alone her plaintive form ascends the sky.

O sing! the water-golds are deepening now,
A hush is come upon the beechen bough;
She shines the while on thee, as saint to
        saint
Sweet interchanged adorings may allow:
Sing, dearest, with that lily throat uplifted;
They are so like, the holy Moon and thou!

43

A MAN said unto his angel:
  " My spirits are fallen thro',
And I cannot carry this battle;
O brother! what shall I do?

"The terrible Kings are on me,
With spears that are deadly bright,
Against me so from the cradle
Do fate and my fathers fight."

Then said to the man his angel:
"Thou wavering, foolish soul,
Back to the ranks! What matter
To win or to lose the whole,

" As judged by the little judges
Who hearken not well, nor see?
Not thus, by the outer issue,
The Wise shall interpret thee.

" Thy will is the very, the only,
The solemn event of things;
The weakest of hearts defying
Is stronger than all these Kings.

" Tho' out of the past they gather,
Mind's Doubt and Bodily Pain,
And pallid Thirst of the Spirit
That is kin to the other twain,

" And Grief, in a cloud of banners,
And ringletted Vain Desires,
And Vice, with the spoils upon him
Of thee and thy beaten sires,

" While Kings of eternal evil
Yet darken the hills about,
Thy part is with broken sabre
To rise on the last redoubt ;

" To fear not sensible failure,
Nor covet the game at all,
But fighting, fighting, fighting,
Die, driven against the wall ! "

45

ALEXANDRIANA

I

I LAID the strewings, sweetest, on thine
    urn;
I lowered the torch, I poured the cup to
    Dis.
Now hushaby, my little child, and learn
Long sleep how good it is.

In vain thy mother prays, wayfaring hence,
Peace to her heart, where only heartaches
    dwell;
But thou more blest, O wild intelligence!
Forget her, and Farewell.

II

Gentle Grecian passing by,
Father of thy peace am I:
Wouldst thou now, in memory,
Give a soldier's flower to me,
Choose the flag I named of yore
Beautiful Worth-dying-for,
That shall wither not, but wave
All the year above my grave.

III

Light thou hast of the moon,
Shade of the dammar-pine,
Here on thy hillside bed;
Fair befall thee, O fair
Lily of womanhood,
Patient long, and at last
Here on thy hillside bed,
Happier: ah, Blæsilla!

49

IV

Two white heads the grasses cover :
Dorcas, and her lifelong lover.
While they graced their country closes
Simply as the brooks and roses,
Where was lot so poor, so trodden,
But they cheered it of a sudden ?
Fifty years at home together,
Hand in hand, they went elsewhither,
Then first leaving hearts behind
Comfortless.   Be thou as kind.

V

Upon thy level tomb, till windy winter dawn,
The fallen leaves delay ;
But plain and pure their trace is, when them-
      selves are torn
From delicate frost away.

As here to transient frost the absent leaf is, such
Thou wert and art to me :
So on my passing life is thy long-passèd touch,
O dear Alcithoë !

VI

Hail, and be of comfort, thou pious Xeno,
Late the urn of many a kinsman wreathing ;
On thine own shall even the stranger offer
Plentiful myrtle.

VII

Here lies one in the earth who scarce of the
      earth was moulded,
Wise Æthalides' son, himself no lover of study,

50

Cnopus, asleep, indoors: the young invincible
    runner.
They from the cliff footpath that see on the
    grave we made him,
Tameless, slant in the wind, the bare and
    beautiful iris,
Stop short, full of delight, and shout forth:
    "See, it is Cnopus
Runs, with white throat forward, over the
    sands to Chalcis!"

VIII

Ere the Ferryman from the coast of spirits
Turn the diligent oar that brought thee thither,
Soul, remember: and leave a kiss upon it
For thy desolate father, for thy sister,
Whichsoever be first to cross hereafter.

IX

Jaffa ended, Cos begun
Thee, Aristeus. Thou wert one
Fit to trample out the sun:
Who shall think thine ardors are
But a cinder in a jar?

X

Me, deep-tressèd meadows, take to your loyal
    keeping,
Hard by the swish of sickles ever in Aulon
    sleeping,
Philophron, old and tired, and glad to be done
    with reaping!

XI

As wind that wasteth the unmarried rose,
And mars the golden breakers in the bay,
Hurtful and sweet from heaven forever blows
Sad thought that roughens all our quiet day;

And elder poets envy while they weep
Ion, whom first the gods to covert brought,
Here under inland olives laid asleep,
Most wise, most happy, having done with
    thought.

XII

Cows in the narrowing August marshes,
Cows in a stretch of water
Motionless,
Neck on neck overlapped and drooping;

These in their troubled and dumb communion,
Thou on the steep bank yonder,
Pastora!
No more ever to lead and love them,

No more ever.   Thine innocent mourners
Pass thy tree in the evening
Heavily,
Hearing another herd-girl calling.

XIII

Praise thou the Mighty Mother for what is
    wrought, not me,
A nameless nothing-caring head asleep against
    her knee.

LONDON:

TWELVE SONNETS

THABOR of England! since my light is short
And faint, O rather by the sun anew
Of timeless passion set my dial true,
That with thy saints and thee I may consort,
And wafted in the calm Chaucerian port
Of poets, seem a little sail long due,
And be as one the call of memory drew
Unto the saddle void since Agincourt!

Not now for secular love's unquiet lease
Receive my soul, who rapt in thee erewhile
Hath broken tryst with transitory things;
But seal with her a marriage and a peace
Eternal, on thine Edward's holy isle,
Above the stormy sea of ended kings.

❦

LIKE bodiless water passing in a sigh, *Fog*
Thro' palsied streets the fatal shadows flow,
And in their sharp disastrous undertow
Suck in the morning sun, and all the sky.
The towery vista sinks upon the eye,
As if it heard the Hebrew bugles blow,
Black and dissolved; nor could the founders know
How what was built so bright should daily die.

Thy mood with man's is broken and blent in,
City of Stains! and ache of thought doth drown

55

Fog   The primitive light in which thy life began;
Great as thy dole is, smirchèd with his sin,
Greater and elder yet the love of man
Full in thy look, tho' the dark visor's down.

❧

*St. Peter-
ad-Vincula*   TOO well I know, pacing the place of awe,
Three queens, young save in trouble,
moulder by;
More in his halo, Monmouth's mocking eye,
The eagle Essex in a harpy's claw;
Seymour and Dudley, and stout heads that
saw
Sundown of Scotland: how with treasons lie
White martyrdoms; rank in a company
Breaker and builder of the eternal law.

Oft as I come, the hateful garden-row
Of ruined roses hanging from the stem,
Where winds of old defeat yet batter them,
Infects me: suddenly must I depart,
Ere thought of men's injustice then and now
Add to these aisles one other broken heart.

❧

*Strikers in
Hyde Park*   A WOOF reversed the fatal shuttles weave,
How slow! but never once they slip the
thread.
Hither, upon the Georgian idlers' tread,
Up spacious ways the lindens interleave,

Clouding the royal air since yester-eve,
Come men bereft of time and scant of bread,
Loud, who were dumb, immortal, who were
    dead,
Thro' the cowed world their kingdom to re-
    trieve.

What ails thee, England? Altar, mart, and
    grange
Dream of the knife by night; not so, not so
The clear Republic waits the general throe,
Along her noonday mountains' open range.
God be with both! for one is young to know
The other's rote of evil and of change.

           ❦

THE cry is at thy gates, thou darling ground, *Changes in*
   Again; for oft ere now thy children went *the Temple*
Beggared and wroth, and parting greeting sent
Some red old alley with a dial crowned;
Some house of honor, in a glory bound
With lives and deaths of spirits excellent;
Some tree rude-taken from his kingly tent
Hard by a little fountain's friendly sound.

O for Virginius' hand, if only that
Maintain the whole, and spoil these spoilings
    soon!
Better the scowling Strand should lose, alas,
Her peopled oasis, and where it was
All mournful in the cleared quadrangle sat
Echo, and ivy, and the loitering moon.

THE evenfall, so slow on hills, hath shot
　Far down into the valley's cold extreme,
Untimely midnight; spire and roof and stream
Like fleeing spectres, shudder and are not.
The Hampstead hollies, from their sylvan plot
Yet cloudless, lean to watch as in a dream,
From chaos climb with many a sudden gleam,
London, one moment fallen and forgot.

Her booths begin to flare; and gases bright
Prick door and window; all her streets ob-
　　scure
Sparkle and swarm with nothing true nor
　　sure,
Full as a marsh of mist and winking light;
Heaven thickens over, Heaven that cannot cure
Her tear by day, her fevered smile by night.

Doves

AH, if man's boast and man's advance be
　vain,
And yonder bells of Bow, loud-echoing home,
And the lone Tree foreknow it, and the Dome,
The monstrous island of the middle main;
If each inheritor must sink again
Under his sires, as falleth where it clomb
Back on the gone wave the disheartened
　　foam? —
I crossed Cheapside, and this was in my brain.

What folly lies in forecasts and in fears!
Like a wide laughter sweet and opportune,

Wet from the fount, three hundred doves of *Doves*
       Paul's
Shook their warm wings, drizzling the golden
       noon,
And in their rain-cloud vanished up the walls.
"God keeps," I said, "our little flock of
       years."

❦

PRAISED be the moon of books! that *In the*
    doth above   *Reading-*
                                           Room of the
A world of men, the fallen Past behold,   *British*
And fill the spaces else so void and cold   *Museum*
To make a very heaven again thereof;
As when the sun is set behind a grove,
And faintly unto nether ether rolled,
All night his whiter image and his mould
Grows beautiful with looking on her love.

Thou therefore, moon of so divine a ray,
Lend to our steps both fortitude and light!
Feebly along a venerable way
They climb the infinite, or perish quite;
Nothing are days and deeds to such as they,
While in this liberal house thy face is bright.

❦

ACROSS the bridge, where in the morning *Sunday*
    blow   *Chimes in*
                                         the City
The wrinkled tide turns homeward, and is fain
Homeward to drag the black sea-goer's chain,
And the long yards by Dowgate dipping low;

59

Across dispeopled ways, patient and slow,
Saint Magnus and Saint Dunstan call in
    vain:
From Wren's forgotten belfries, in the rain,
Down the blank wharves the dropping octaves
    go.

Forbid not these! Tho' no man heed, they
    shower
A subtle beauty on the empty hour,
From all their dark throats aching and out-
    blown;
Aye in the prayerless places welcome most,
Like the last gull that up a naked coast
Deploys her white and steady wing, alone.

❧

WHEN, after dawn, the lordly houses hide
    Till you fall foul of it, some piteous
    guest,
Some girl the damp stones gather to their
    breast,
Her gold hair rough, her rebel garment wide,
Who sleeps, with all that luck and life de-
    nied
Camped round, and dreams how seaward and
    southwest
Blue over Devon farms the smoke-rings rest,
And sheep and lambs ascend the lit hillside,

Dear, of your charity, speak low, step soft,
Pray for a sinner. Planet-like and still,
Best hearts of all are sometimes set aloft

Only to see and pass, nor yet deplore *A Porch*
Even Wrong itself, crowned Wrong inscruta- *in Belgra-*
    ble, *via.*
Which cannot not have been for evermore.

❦

MANY a musing eye returns to thee, *York Stairs*
    Against the lurid street disconsolate,
Who kept in green domains thy bridal state,
With young tide-waters leaping at thy knee;
And lest the ravening smoke, and enmity,
Corrode thee quite, thy lover sighs, and
        straight
Desires thee safe afar, too graceful gate!
Throned on a terrace of the Boboli.

Nay, nay, thy use is here. Stand queenly thus
Till the next fury; teach the time and us
Leisure and will to draw a serious breath:
Not wholly where thou art the soul is cowed,
Nor the fooled capital proclaims aloud
Barter is god, while Beauty perisheth.

❦

WHERE the bales thunder till the day is *In the*
    done, *Docks*
And the wild sounds with wilder odors cope;
Where over crouching sail and coiling rope,
Lascar and Moor along the gangway run;
Where stifled Thames spreads in the pallid sun,
A hive of anarchy from slope to slope;

Flag of my birth, my liberty, my hope,
I see thee at the masthead, joyous one !

O thou good guest ! So oft as, young and warm,
To the home-wind thy hoisted colors bound,
Away, away from this too thoughtful ground,
Sated with human trespass and despair,
Thee only, from the desert, from the storm,
A sick mind follows into Eden air.

www.ingramcontent.com/pod-product-compliance
Lightning Source LLC
Chambersburg PA
CBHW022017080426
42733CB00007B/630